china contemporary

photographs by MICHAEL FREEMAN
text by XIAO DAN WANG

With 285 illustrations in color

Preceding pages: The reception desk at a publishing house in Beijing was designed by Liang Jian Guo in the form of a traditional typesetting block (**page 1**). The boardwalk on the edge of Xuanwu Lake in Nanjing (**pages 2–3**). **This page:** The Shanghai World Financial Centre, at 492 metres, is the tallest building in China as of 2008. **Following pages:** Measuring 700 by 27 metres, the length of a city block, Asia's largest LED screen displays an animated underwater scene over The Place, a shopping mall in Beijing's central business district (**pages 8–9**). Visitors at Shanghai MoCA viewing a work by Wang Xiao Hui entitled *My Last Hundred Years*, 2006 (**pages 10–11**). A Qing Dynasty merchant's house in Anhui province. With few windows to the outside, these houses featured 'light wells' over a central courtyard, which was the centre of family activity (**pages 12–13**). A four-storey circular clan house in the southern province of Fujian, one of several thousand fortified buildings in a style unique to the area. Dating back to the 13th century, they were built to provide communal protection (**pages 14–15**).

First published in 2009 in hardcover in the United States of America by Thames & Hudson Inc., 500 Fifth Avenue, New York, New York 10110

thamesandhudsonusa.com

Library of Congress Catalog Card Number 2008900092

ISBN 978-0-500-51418-4

Printed and bound in Singapore by Tien Wah Press

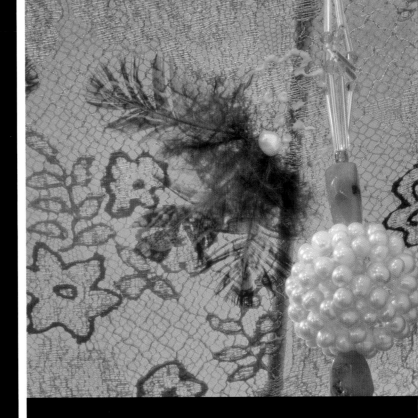
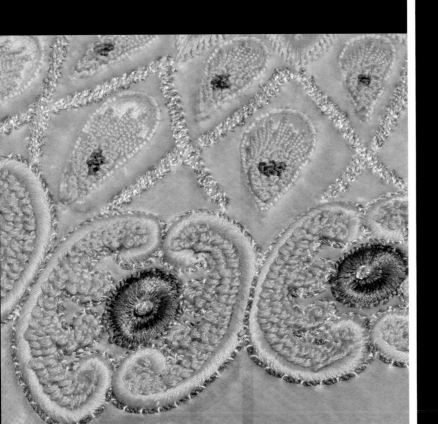

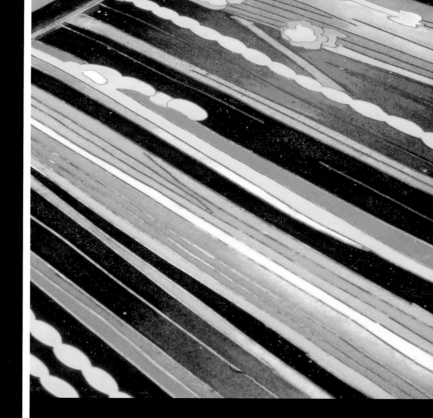

CONVERSION
128

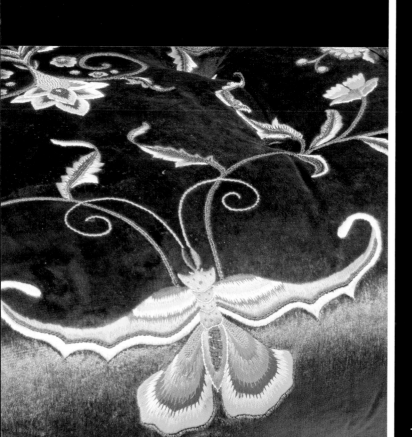

crossover
202

Contemporary China is undergoing a second cultural revolution – a result of, and a complement to, its expanding economy. Exciting new developments in architecture and in the decorative and fine arts are characterized by a willingness to experiment, both in design and materials. Some of the buildings and homes illustrated on the pages that follow have taken the traditional Chinese design vernacular and reinvigorated it by giving it a contemporary form or by expressing it in unexpected ways.

I. M. Pei, for instance, has designed the distinguished Suzhou Museum in a distinctly modernist style, but using the colour schemes of traditional Suzhou housing. Other examples show a distinctly Western influence, expressed in the time-honoured materials of Chinese craftsmanship: brick, wood and paper. Whatever the emphasis of their design principles, all the buildings and interiors in this book have a distinctive air of visual excitement and vibrancy: dazzling domestic installations in former Communist-era blocks; renovations of early 20th-century factories and apartments; and the construction of new homes by architects, artists and designers who still demand the highest standards of traditional Chinese craftsmanship. But whatever their function, style or materials, all of these projects are utterly contemporary.

By the early 1990s, the privatization of property ownership in China meant that people started investing time and money in the look of their homes. As the Chinese economy and property market continue to blossom, the words *zhuang xiu* (renovation) have become part of daily vocabulary.

Today, people normally buy properties in which only the essential structures are provided. Areas are assigned a function but remain wholly unfurnished, giving the owners freedom to experiment. This has resulted in the birth of a whole generation of self-styled interior designers. Recently, Chinese blogger Tang Liang won the National Interior Design Diary Award with his online DIY interior design blog, which receives five thousand hits a day and has been made into a book. He says, 'I don't trust your average interior designer – they are only interested in making money, not in designing my house. They won't take as much care of my house as I do. It is my life, and I design it.'

Modern Chinese architecture and design are influenced by both modern Western styles and traditional Chinese principles. Degree-level interior design courses have only been available in Chinese art and design institutes for just over a decade, which is a very short time to assimilate a century and a half of modern Western design, and an even shorter time to comprehend five thousand years of Chinese culture and tradition, which came to a halt in the first Cultural Revolution.

Many of the homes and commercial premises presented in this book are owned by artists or designers, who have played an important role in their creation. Having lived outside China for a few years, I was surprised by the fearless quality shown in some of these designs. A recent article in *The Economist* said, 'The 19th century belonged to Paris, the 20th century belonged to New York, and the 21st century belongs to London.' Will the second half of the 21st century belong to Beijing?

Most of the billboards around Beijing's ever- expanding ring roads show property advertisements selling an array of desirable lifestyles: Mediterranean Chic, Silicon Valley, New-China Living. We are living in a time in which anything seems possible, and people are eager to experiment. These are certainly extraordinary times for anyone involved in architecture and design.

Continuity

China's five thousand years of history have given its people a rich cultural heritage – architectural, literary, artistic and philosophical. Even though the country suffered a traumatic culture shock during the middle and late 20th century, its traditions remained strong, and robust economic growth in this new era has given it another opportunity to blossom. The locations in this section of the book make clear cultural references to the past, although they have been created for today's modern urban lifestyle. In these designs, cultural continuity is about re-examining and reinterpreting the traditional aesthetic and ethical values and adding today's contemporary stamp.

Chinese traditional culture is very much influenced by Confucianism, Taoism and Buddhism, and their values have a profound impact on Chinese art and culture to this day. Moderation and syncretism are the core values of Confucianism. Its philosophy emphasizes the unity and harmony between man and his surroundings. This unity is the fundamental principle of traditional Chinese design and it is scrupulously observed by Chinese artists and designers. The Suzhou Museum designed by I. M. Pei extends the principle to a union of old and new styles. The design takes the traditional colours and shapes of Suzhou architecture but uses modern forms and materials. It blends into the historical surroundings seamlessly, yet is clearly a product of the 21st century.

The mystery and the ethereal beauty of nature are the essence of Taoism. The Tao – the way or order of the universe – follows nature, which is abstract and cannot be logically explained. In terms of design, it is often embodied in the rich spatial expressions of interleaving and interpenetration: for example, by bringing external views inside through windows or doors and using flexible partitions so that decoration is shared between different spaces. Traditional colours and materials, as well as long-established visual elements, are used to create an environment that brings spiritual peace and tranquillity. Deng Kun Yen's garden in Shanghai is a perfect example. The moon gates take the traditional form typical of a southern Chinese garden design (p. 40); they frame and connect a sequence of different views. Deng uses the moon shape to reflect the philosophical

beliefs of Buddhism and his own withdrawal from worldliness. However, he wants to signify that there are new meanings, beyond the sense of peace, to this traditional visual element.

Nirvana – enlightenment or release – is the ultimate goal of Buddhism. The less prescriptive the belief, the more room there is for the imagination. Only when one has a sense of the absolute minimum, can one have the maximum freedom to imagine and reflect. A simple and minimalist colour palette is the contemporary expression of this ancient philosophy. For instance, the Green T. House has an all-white theme, while its interpretation of traditional Ming furniture connects with an authentic Chinese lifestyle, without being in any way conventional.

Ever since the middle of the 19th century, the question of national identity has loomed large in Chinese cultural, historical, political and economic discourse. Following the reforms in the late 1970s and the decline of socialism, questions of cultural and historical continuity are once again the focus of heated debate in China. The 'socialism with Chinese characteristics' formula implies a reconciliation of modernity and tradition, of global and local. It leads inevitably to a re-expression of China's tradition and national characteristics, as well as to the creation of a new historical consciousness focused on the present era.

HOT LOFT RESTAURANT (BEIJING)

The Hot Loft occupies a space within the Coco Building in the Chaoyang district of East Beijing. It was originally opened as The Loft by the owner, Lin Tian Mu, in 1999; after its immediate success he decided to commission a complete makeover by the Japanese architect Sakae Miura, who also designed the People Restaurant – Space 6 in Shanghai.

An all-glass elevator takes diners up to the restaurant on the dimly lit fifth floor, the door to which can only be opened by passing a hand over a large cooking vessel in an illuminated glass case. This cauldron is a *ding* (or *ting*), a type of cooking pot used in China since antiquity. Resting on either three or four legs – and often referred to as a tripod – the *ding* is a simple but important symbol of power. In Chinese tradition, possession of an ancient tripod indicated the elevated social status of the owner, and was often associated with dominion over the land. In the Hot Loft, the tripod is the centrepiece of the restaurant's themed design, focusing attention upon the signature dish, hotpot, a soup served in a communal pot. The simple act of lifting the pot's lid carries with it a resonance of ritual significance.

Within the restaurant, the different areas are clearly defined; along one wall is the open kitchen behind a metre-wide stainless-steel bar counter that continues through the whole space. The chefs wear all-white uniforms and masks and go about preparing food as if in some futuristic laboratory. Carved wooden screens separate the dining area and the kitchen, and also grant a degree of privacy to the rectangular dining units. At one end of the dining room is a long table that can seat twenty-six people at a time. The background colour of the walls and ceiling is a subdued dark grey.

A collection of different tripods are displayed in two glass cabinets, including a stainless-steel hotpot designed by Lin Tian Mu, owner of the minimalist chic restaurant Hot Loft (*right*).

Overleaf: An all-glass elevator takes diners to the restaurant on the fifth floor of the Coco Building. A large tripod in a glass case glows in the entranceway to the restaurant, alerting visitors to the hotpot theme. Only when a hand is passed over the tripod will the heavy metal door slide open to reveal the restaurant behind (*left*). The Ming Dynasty columns beneath the bar counter are decorated with cloud patterns (*right*).

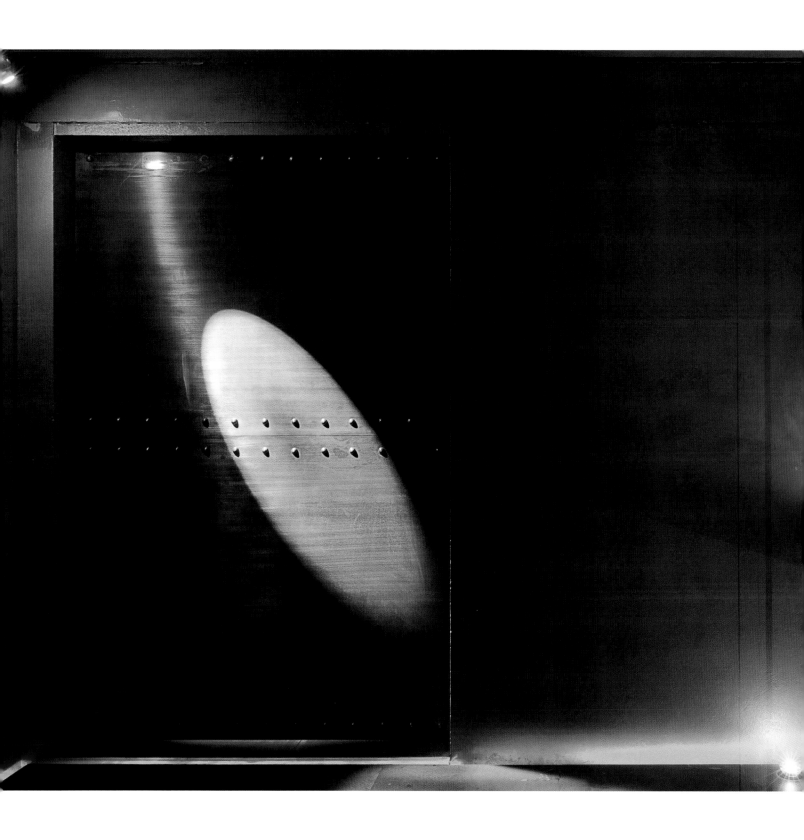

GREEN T. HOUSE (BEIJING)

When JinR opened Green T. House in the Workers' Gymnasium West area in Beijing in 1997, she fulfilled a long-held ambition to manage a large teahouse. The initial design for the building included a vast space for the teahouse, but she wanted everything to be longer, taller and generally bigger. Every dimension of the interior was extended as far as possible, and mirrors were placed throughout the building – on walls, tables and chairs and around the bar – to create a sense of spaciousness. The presence of so many mirrors, however, initially discouraged custom as they made the teahouse look like a shop where nothing appeared to be for sale. A *feng shui* master eventually solved the problem by removing the mirrors from behind the bar, which is positioned across from the main entrance: in traditional *feng shui* theory, a mirror opposite a door repels people. Now, a decade after it first opened, Green T. House is a thriving venue. A-list celebrities are drawn by the restaurant's soothing ambience and the successful fusion of a traditional teahouse social atmosphere with a modern culinary experience.

Tall steel screens, which resemble carved wood, are used to divide the main dining area at the Green T. House from a quiet area featuring a 'Buddha bed' where people can sit and relax.

White-painted stairs (*below*) lead to the office of the
Green T. House. All of the office furniture is also painted
white (*opposite*).

A mirrored table and Ming-style chairs, lengthened and curved beyond their traditional proportions, retain the elegance of the models upon which they were based. JinR used steel to create a frame for the chairs, and their exteriors were then covered with highly polished wood. The chair seats were further reinforced with steel plates to support the heavy steel backs (*opposite*).

In an extension of the dining room, JinR created an alternative seating option by placing a large rough tree branch along the wall and inviting guests to sit upon it. Smaller branches, which are painted white, are used as ceiling decorations (*below*).

GREEN T. HOUSE LIVING (BEIJING)

With the addition of a newly constructed complex 15,000 metres square, Green T. House Living builds upon the success of Green T. House. It includes a second teahouse, a full restaurant, an art gallery, a spa and a villa, which serves as an exclusive luxury hotel.

The all-white main room of the restaurant was a particularly challenging design problem for architect Jiang Tao, as the owner stipulated that there should be no visible support columns. To achieve this, Jiang increased the size of the beams and concealed the vertical support elements in the structure of the front wall. Specially commissioned white tiles from the ceramics city of Jing De Zheng line the main space. The pavilion style of the restaurant borrows from Qin Dynasty architecture, and by placing the kitchen out of sight underground, Jiang has created a dramatic view of the surrounding country-side. Terraced courtyards of white stone lead to the spa, where traditional Chinese therapies are offered. Beyond that, an open-plan guest house welcomes visitors for longer stays.

Two historical eras in particular influenced Jiang's design for the Green T. House Living complex. Inspiration for the structure of the buildings came from the simple architectural style of the Warring States Period (5th century BC to the unification of China by the Qin Dynasty in 221 BC). Highlights throughout the buildings were influenced by Tang Dynasty (AD 690–705) details, such as the peony – the national flower during the Tang Dynasty – cast on every tile in the dining room (*right*).

Special paper lanterns, hand-painted by JinR's sister, were designed in the shape of water drops (*opposite*).

Preceding pages: In contrast to the very stylized chairs at Green T. House, the design of these chairs is particularly reserved. Bold gestures have been avoided, while sheer comfort has been given precedence; the white chair was remodelled seven times before it met with the designer's approval. The large birdcage is JinR's own design.

A gift shop in the basement displays objects designed by JinR (*below*). Designer Jiang was very economical with space, and decided to place all of the non-restaurant functions underground, including the gift shop, the kitchen and the bathrooms. These areas are connected to the restaurant by an underground tunnel, which also leads to the tearoom (*opposite*).

反觀
REFLEXIVITY

DENG KUN YEN STUDIO AND GARDEN (SHANGHAI)

The Da Yang architecture studio of Deng Kun Yen is located in an old industrial warehouse in the Yangpu district of Shanghai, on the Huangpu River. It is part of the Shanghai creative industrial park that Deng helped to establish. Every effort was made to make as few changes as possible to the three-storey structure in the course of its renovation. Original features, like the big round holes in the loft space, were retained and reflected in three additional moon gates on the first floor. These circular passageways represent the three key concepts of Taoism: original essence, original energy and original awareness.

Outside the studio, two additional moon gates welcome visitors into the garden. All the original large trees have been retained, and are now connected by a network of bamboo canes and hanging flowers.

Flower baskets (*above*) hang from steel structures in the garden, also viewed here from the roof terrace (*above left*). Grey bricks brought from other building sites were reused to make walls and circles on the main garden square, as well as two moon gates (*left*). A large mirror has been placed opposite the second moon gate with a sign above it, which reads 'Reflect'. This is a joke revealing Deng's concern about the lack of intellectual property protection in China, and is intended to send a message of reflection to those who would imitate his work.

An overview of Deng's garden during lunch break; the horizontal bamboo canes contrast with the vertical trees (*opposite*). Posters or flower baskets can be hung from them (*top right*). Slogans from the original factory building have been left untouched, still promoting the messages of unity and progress. Old tiles line the garden, sometimes placed face up (*above right*) or stacked sideways (*above left*).

Two moon gates face each other in Deng's garden; beyond is the mirror pictured on pages 40–41(*right*).

Overleaf: In his office, Deng uses a bamboo chair in a style often seen in southern China (*left*). The lobby of the studio is visible beyond a moon gate (*right*). Among the original features retained were the big round apertures in the loft, known as 'cat holes' and originally intended as a means of access for people doing building work.

Preceding pages: The ground-floor entrance to Deng's studio *(above left)*; the garden can be seen from inside the studio *(below left)*. Deng brought in an old steel factory room to use as his office on the first floor; this was the only extension to the original warehouse building. Skylight windows were opened up in the ceiling, so that the sun could shine on a dozen silver glass bulbs hanging among the beams. They slowly rotate 360 degrees to reflect sunlight into every corner of the room. This is a modern interpretation of an old Buddhist metaphor that the Buddha distributes his glory to all beings *(right)*.

To create a more convivial atmosphere for social gatherings, candleholders were installed in the original brick walls of the building *(left)*.

SUZHOU MUSEUM (SUZHOU)

The city of Suzhou, in Jiangsu province, is proud of its gardens. Two of the most beautiful gardens, listed as Unesco World Heritage sites, surround the city's museum of Chinese art. Designed by I. M. Pei, a native of the region, the museum complex was opened in 2006 and effectively combines the traditional and the modern. Pitched roofs and flyaway eaves are evocative of the region's traditional architectural style, but are constructed in entirely contemporary materials: wooden beams and rafters have been replaced with steel. The main entrance, lobby and museum garden are in the centre of the complex. The west wing, which terminates in an indoor lotus pond, houses the main exhibition area, and the east wing includes a gallery of contemporary art and a teahouse. As in the traditional gardens of Suzhou, water, footbridges and pavilions act as unifying elements throughout the complex.

The museum uses traditional Suzhou architectural vocabulary, including patios and a white and grey colour palette. However, the usual grey tiles on the arched roof and window frames have been replaced with grey granite to give consistent colour and texture. The buildings retain a traditional ascending form, but with added rectangular and triangular extensions to the roofs (*below and opposite*).

Overleaf: A steel and glass pavilion shimmers in the water (*left*). Details of plants, ponds, rocks and a waterfall within the carefully landscaped gardens at the museum (*right*).

A walkway over the lotus pond connects one wing
of the museum to the other (*below*).

The pavilion overlooking the lotus pond (*left*).

The museum is full of fascinating visual details: a view from the pagoda (*above*); a walkway lined with stands of bamboo skirts the exterior of the museum (*opposite, left*); a garden decorated with stones that are meant to resemble mountains (*opposite, right*).

This villa is part of a 46-unit, low-density residential development. The design is intended to create a contemporary residential building for the newly wealthy families of modern China. The living and dining rooms are surrounded by floor-to-ceiling glass walls, which reflect the mild climate in this part of China and are perfect for connecting inner and outer space, allowing light to flow from one room to the next (*opposite*).

The living and dining rooms occupy a two-storey glass house-within-a-house, shielded to the north by an angled, interlocking grille of aluminium tubes and shaded on the south side by a screen of wooden slats. The screen filters out strong sunlight, casting soft light and shadows in the dining room (*below*).

PUDONG VILLAS (SHANGHAI)

The commission to design an unconventional villa was an opportunity that the Hong Kong architect Rocco Yim could not resist. Part of a low-density residential development on the east bank of the Huangpu River, deep in the Pudong district, the villa represented Rocco's chance to update traditional Chinese concepts in terms of today's living patterns. The project was carried out in collaboration with the architecture and interior design studio CL3.

A low, whitewashed wall encloses the entire complex, shielding residents from the noise of the street. Water is a central element within the whole design, owing to the riverside location of the development, and the resulting villa is a contemporary interpretation of the traditional architecture found in the water villages of southern China.

The main bedroom contains a modern reinterpretation of a traditional Ming-style bed (*opposite*). Wooden slats line the bathroom (*right*), which is decorated with other natural materials, including marble (*below*).

A hallway gallery inside the villa. In the past, Chinese families were very closely knit and lived according to certain traditional values, including close communication between different generations of the same family living in one house. This hallway serves both to connect the different sections of the villa, and to separate them for privacy (*left*).

Overleaf: The overall design employed a contemporary minimalist architectural vocabulary, using materials such as glass, aluminium and marble. However, these materials also reflect the traditional Chinese characteristics of tranquillity, modesty and simplicity.

FUMIN ROAD APARTMENT (SHANGHAI)

This one-bedroom apartment is in a building dating from the 1920s. In 2005, the interior was redesigned by the firm sciSKEW Collaborative to maximize the use of the limited living area through a modern interpretation of the time-honoured Chinese technique of using wooden cabinets to divide space. The result is a highly functional and surprisingly domestic dwelling. Simple materials – walnut, plywood and vinyl floor tiles – were used in the construction of the individual fittings. One interesting aspect of the construction process was the manner in which the computer-generated design was relayed to the local building crew, who were unable to understand sciSKEW's initial drawings. Eventually, a single, precisely annotated paper model was used to convey the designers' vision to the construction team.

The previous owners of the apartment used furniture – in particular, wooden cabinets – to divide space into differentiated living zones. The designers used this as raw material with which to begin their work. The original configuration of the wooden cabinetry was mapped into the computer, and the new continuous cabinet references the original arrangement, but incorporates modern living requirements (*below*).

The walnut and plywood cabinets were built using computer-generated models. Many necessary domestic functions are contained within the units, including air conditioning, lighting, seating, wardrobes and storage (*right*).

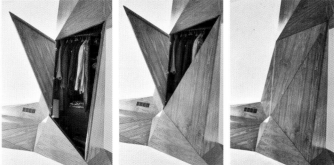

The bedroom also contains sculptural cabinets, which incorporate the bed frame and full-size wardrobes (*opposite*). A view of the other side of the bedroom (*above*); tables and stools are designed in the same style as the built-in wardrobes (*right*).

A LANE HOUSE (SHANGHAI)

This traditional house, in Nanhui Road in central Shanghai, is the third lane house to be redesigned by the architects of the sciSKEW Collaborative. Their imaginative approach to design prompts them to explore and unearth stories embedded within their sites. In the case of this house, altered and given additional space in 2006, the history of the building and its previous occupants became the raw material for an architectural experiment.

The typical Shanghai lane house is based on a modular floor plan, and almost always faces south. This usually creates several north-facing pavilion rooms, stacked above the main level. These rooms are often small, dark and relatively useless, but in this design they have been unified into a continuous sequence spiralling up from the ground floor to the roof terrace on the third floor, which results in an especially spacious and bright lane house.

As much of the original 1930s building as possible has been restored and preserved, and wherever changes have been made, the new materials were chosen to match those of the period in which the house was built. The front and back gardens of the site were landscaped in a more contemporary manner and visually connected by French doors on either side of the living area.

The back garden is embellished with a mosaic footpath (*below*). A glass-enclosed hallway also serves as a storage area (*right*). Both front and back gardens have been re-landscaped in an entirely contemporary manner (*opposite*).

The so-called 'pavilion rooms', stacked half a storey above the main floor levels, have been opened up and turned into useful spaces, like this bathroom (*opposite*). Taking up two standard bays, this lane house is made especially bright by the French doors that open on to the gardens (*below*).

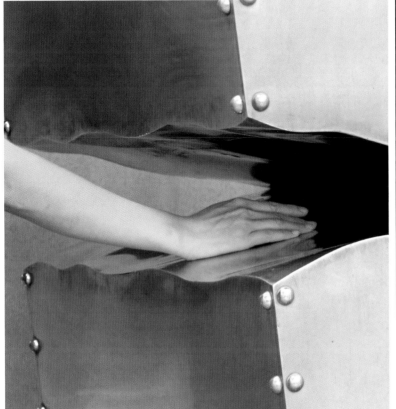

PEOPLE RESTAURANT – SPACE 6 (SHANGHAI)

Surrounded by academic buildings, the People Restaurant is located near the corner of Yue Yang Road and Yong Jia Road in a quiet neighbourhood in Shanghai. The three-storey building stands among bamboo trees and paulownias. There is no sign outside, so the first challenge of eating at the restaurant is identifying the building; the second is discovering how to open the stainless-steel door. Once the hidden palm-operated security pad has been located, a long walkway through a bamboo garden awaits beyond the entrance.

Between the first and second set of stainless-steel doors is a bamboo garden with a long pebble-bordered path, marked out for hopscotch (*opposite*). Outside the entrance door, two steel blocks (*above*) conceal the palm-operated entrance control (*below*).

Overleaf: A look through the thirty round holes in the doors reveals the bamboo garden (*left*). Designer Sakae Miura's inspiration came from one of the most famous poems by poet, politician and artist Su Shi (1037–1101), which includes a vision of a Moon Palace made of jade (*centre*). Sakae uses only stainless steel, cement and glass to express his contemporary interpretation of the Moon Palace. Passing through a second set of sliding steel doors and a glass entranceway, diners finally arrive at a hallway leading to the restaurant itself (*right*).

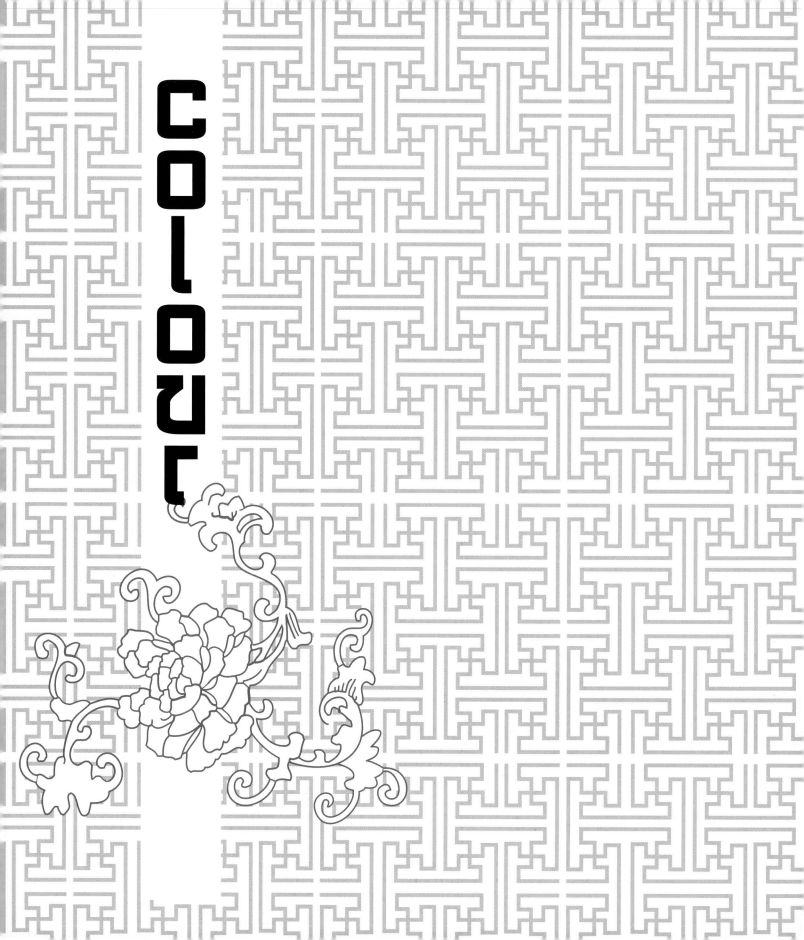

COLOUR

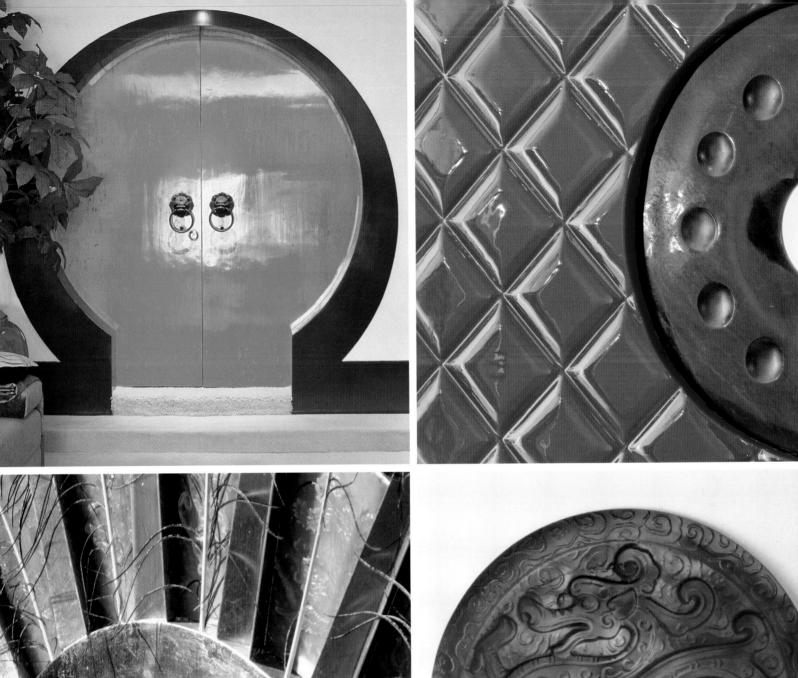

When we enter any space, much of our attention is focused on colour. Whether we are aware of it or not, colour and light affect us physically and emotionally in all our daily activities. If handled well, they can give a space a dramatic face-lift at minimal cost compared with other interior design methods or techniques. The ways in which colour is used represent a home owner's personality and character, and gender, age and education level all affect colour preferences.

Ethnic tradition is another factor. In ancient China, people believed that certain elements – water, fire, wood, metal and earth – were the source of everything in nature, including colour. These elements corresponded to black, red, greenish-blue, white and yellow. People selected their attire, food, transportation and housing according to the natural changes in the seasons, which are also reflected in the theory of colours. Red symbolizes good fortune, excitement and joy. It is often used at weddings and typically at Spring Festival, where red couplets are found outside every house. During the Chinese New Year, everything is red, from paper decorations cut with lucky patterns to fireworks. In Western culture, white is the colour of purity, which brings peace and comfort. Although white has these same associations in China, it is also the colour of mourning. People wear all-white clothes and headbands at funerals. In Taoism, the concept of infinity is expressed in the intertwined black *yin* and white *yang*, and black and white are considered to be the origin of all colours. Yellow is the colour of the earth and is regarded as the most important of all colours. It is, therefore, the colour of royalty, used for the robes of emperors and the decor of royal palaces. Only the royal family could wear yellow in ancient China. Greenish-blue symbolizes spring and vitality. In one example in this section, Zhong Ya Ling's apartment, these traditional colour themes have been translated into an East-meets-West arrangement. Red and gold (yellow) fill the master bedroom with warmth and cosiness. Light blue and pale yellow make the guest room calm and refreshing.

Geographical location and climate also affect colour preferences. In northern Chinese villages, young girls prefer bright-coloured dresses – red, sky-blue and vivid yellow – to brighten the long, dark, cold winters. In southern China, people prefer to wear white or light-coloured clothes due to the extremely hot and humid weather. Colour can be used not only to adjust people's emotions and sense of physical well-being, but also to respond to the demands of the environment. For example, the Huan Bi Tang Gallery in Beijing, designed by Zhong Song, has a south-facing gallery, which gets extremely hot in the summer. Zhong's white leaf-screened hallway creates a tranquil and dynamic breathing space that is almost alive. Its colour and the amount of shade constantly change as the sun moves. The hallway also serves as a light filter to reduce the heat inside the room. In Zhong's own apartment, he used only black and white elements to divide space. A black wooden structure more than two metres tall is used throughout the apartment as a unifying element. In the entrance hall, it incorporates built-in wardrobes. It then continues into the kitchen, where it turns into cabinets, flowing onward into the living room and becoming a wine bar. After that, it serves as doors to the guest bedroom and bathroom. Ultimately, the structure becomes the master bedroom wardrobe, additionally supporting an upper floor within the room.

Quite a few of the design examples gathered in this section have a white theme. An all-white setting provides a neutral stage for the colourful decorations on display. More importantly, in public spaces, such as the office of the magazine publisher Trends, white enhances the space and shifts attention from the rooms to the people who enter them. As the designer Liang Jian Guo says, 'Without people, there are no trends.' In another essay in white, designers Zhang Zi Hui and Chen Yi Lang have created a contemporary, spacious and practical home for their client by combining different textures, shades, forms and functions, all in white. The smooth, self-levelling white epoxy flooring links together the three floors of the apartment. A white column has been added to divide the entrance hall and living area. One wall is irregularly divided vertically and horizontally to create different types of shadow, giving depth and extra dimension to the surface.

This version of the Chinese moon gate leads to a master bedroom in a Shanghai apartment; the colour indicates happiness and well-being (*opposite, above left*). In the same apartment this multi-coloured dragon decoration adorns a glass door (*opposite, below right*). A detail from a jade and lacquer screen in the collection at Pearl Lam's Contrast Gallery (*opposite, above right*); this peacock feather is another detail from a work in the same collection (*opposite, below left*).

ZHONG YA LING APARTMENT (SHANGHAI)

This twenty-third-floor apartment is located on a bank of the Huangpu River, Shanghai's largest river, and the division line between the eastern and western parts of the city. The building is sited at a 90-degree bend in the river, and as a result the apartment has an extraordinary panoramic view.

The interior design is based upon the exchange of aesthetic ideals between East and West, and plays upon the owner's position as the wife of the chairman of the Swiss–Chinese Chamber of Commerce. For instance, the bright red moon gate takes its form from a combination of the traditional Chinese garden archway and the last letter of the Greek alphabet, omega, by way of a reference to the logo for Omega, the Swiss watchmaker.

This moon gate leads to a living room, which has a stunning view of the Huangpu River.

A gold lacquer screen, decorated with black ink bamboo drawings, rises behind the bed in the master bedroom. The lamps were custom made for the apartment, and add light to the warmth generated by the red and gold colour scheme (*above*).

Light blue and pale yellow create a calm and refreshing atmosphere in a guest bedroom. This room also contains a gold lacquer screen, which has been painted with a detail from a famous Chinese painting, *Along the River During the Qingming Festival*, by the Song Dynasty artist Zhang Zeduan (1085–1145) (**below**).

In a hallway leading to the bathroom (*left*), organically dyed Tibetan wool carpets add colour to the white marble floor (*below left*).

Other bedrooms (*below and opposite*) are characterized by sumptuous colours, with gold and red predominating.

The living room (*left*) is carpeted with a number of antique Chinese rugs. The floor-to-ceiling window has a panoramic view of the Pudong riverside.

The dining area is decorated with antique Chinese furniture; each of the lamps was commissioned for the apartment (*above*).

The focal point in the main living room is an all-white antique ceramic oven. It was originally in a castle in Switzerland, but Zhong had it dismantled and shipped to Shanghai, where a Swiss technician rebuilt it (*opposite*).

A WHITE APARTMENT (BEIJING)

This minimalist apartment – all-white with modernist furniture – is arranged over four floors. The owners, who have strong connections in the media and IT industries, wanted a space in which they could entertain, but which would also provide substantial accommodation for their family.

The designers of the apartment, Zhang Zi Hui and Chen Yi Lang, are both graduates of the prestigious Central Academy of Fine Arts, Beijing. They found that the original structure defined the various areas quite well but that certain changes had to be made to ensure a feeling of continuity within the apartment. A ceiling and column, for instance, were introduced in the entrance hall to indicate the separation of living and dining areas. On the second floor, a child's room connects with an adjoining room reserved for grandparents, reaffirming the closeness of the generations in the traditional Chinese family.

An inventive wine rack is a connecting element between the living room and a children's play room (*opposite*). A top-floor office space is illuminated by skylights, and provides space for two desks (*right*).

The dining area and the living room are separated by a curving ceiling element and a column in the entrance hall. The three-dimensional plasterwork makes the wall decorative as well as functional (*opposite*).

A view of the master bedroom (*below left*).

The living room has a coffee table designed for the apartment by Zhang Zi Hui, who also created the black and grey artwork on the wall (*below centre*).

The staircase leading to the second floor is decorated with a digital print, another work of art by Zhang (*below right*).

TRENDS PUBLISHING HOUSE (BEIJING)

Trends is one of the largest commercial publishing houses in China with thirteen monthly magazines, including *National Geographic Traveler*, *Cosmopolitan*, *Marie Claire* and *Harper's Bazaar*. The company was established in 1993 and has experienced and recorded the vast changes of lifestyle in contemporary China, reflected in the company's own rapid growth. Trends was founded by Wu Hong and Liu Jiang in buildings around a small courtyard, but today it has offices that extend over nine floors of a building in Beijing's central business district.

The publishers' main objective in commissioning new offices was to encourage Trends to grow more quickly. Architect Liang Jian Guo responded to the challenge by designing a space that improves efficiency at all levels by providing Trends employees with a stylish and relaxing place to work. He noted that the pace of work in the magazine publishing industry is extremely rapid and stressful, so it became a priority to create a friendly, hospitable environment where staff could feel happy and healthy. Because Trends shares Liang's focus on employee well-being, the company invested in a 500-square-metre gymnasium as part of the new design.

In order to create a substantial reception area, two floors were opened up to incorporate a ceiling 7 metres above the floor. The reception floor includes a gallery and a replica of the original Trends courtyard office space. This courtyard reminds people how far Trends has come, and some of the original employees were moved to tears when it was first unveiled.

In the all-white recreation hall, it is hard not to notice the colour-changing chandelier, made of optical fibre and crystal. Its shape cleverly reproduces the Trends logo: a full point encircling a comma.

A hallway leads to the human resources department at Trends, which welcomes visitors with a bright yellow and green wall composed of various human figures. This playful design is echoed in the signs indicating the bathrooms along the main hallway. Rather than relying on standard male and female figures, the designers came up with the idea of large faces painted with the traditional makeup of performers at the Beijing Opera, which are realized as intricate mosaics.

The sculpture hanging from the ceiling represents the gatherings in a folded magazine. The plaster construction has the added benefit of being fireproof (**opposite**).

Each magazine has a unique sign reflecting the publication's individual brand. The design for *Harper's Bazaar* (**top**) was hollow-cut in plywood and then filled in with red roses. The *Esquire* department is identified by a more masculine, rugged grey sign (**above left**), while the sign for the Trends gallery is composed of stylized characters articulating the company's values (**above right**).

華夏地理

時尚COSMOPOLITAN

Commissioned artwork can be seen throughout the building and is reflected in the mirrored ceiling (*opposite and far left*).

The *National Geographic* sign references nature with a textured design made of straw (*above left*). A bright pink sign for *Cosmopolitan* indicates the magazine's young female readership (*below left*).

HUAN BI TANG GALLERY (BEIJING)

Known to Western collectors as the China Blue Gallery, this exhibition space is located in the central Chaoyang district of Beijing. It was established in 2002 and now ranks among the elite galleries showing Chinese art. The space devoted to exhibitions is one of the largest in China.

The interior of the building includes an office, a library and a multi-functional area for special events, and was designed by the artist Zhong Song. His idea was to build a sculptural space with which people could interact and which would connect all of the various functional spaces. The centrepiece of the design is a hallway lined with a sculptural sequence of carved leaves, which creates complex patterns of light, and acts as a cooling device in the hot summers.

Artist Zhong Song designed the curved wooden hallway at the gallery with a computer program, and then used a digital cutting process to produce each of the different pieces. The various sections were painted with gloss paint, and assembled to form the structure. When sunlight shines into the gallery, the wooden panels act like leaves, creating a dappled play of light on the floor. As the sun moves around the building, the shadows inside the hallway follow, giving the impression that the space is alive and constantly in motion.

Lights hidden in the panels along the hallway create a welcoming atmosphere. Their reflection on the smooth floor lights the walkway (*left*).

The second floor of the building houses the office, a library and an exhibition area (*opposite*).

LAN CLUB (BEIJING)

The Lan Club, which occupies an entire floor of a skyscraper in central Beijing, is a lavish example of the new internationalism pervading Chinese culture and design. This massive venue is named for restaurateur Zhan Lan, and is the crowning jewel in her successful South Beauty restaurant chain. The club is a complex of oyster and wine bars, cigar rooms, shops, galleries and thirty-five private VIP rooms designed to resemble Mongolian tents.

The interior design and the detailing of the contents are the work of Philippe Starck, inspired by the aesthetics of the private art collections of the Louis XV period. The overwhelming feeling of luxury and exclusivity is achieved largely through the careful selection of the furnishings. More than three thousand articles of furniture and tableware were handmade in France and Italy by craftsmen who work exclusively for Starck. Thirty display cabinets full of colourful objects play up the baroque feel of the surroundings, and draw attention to the uniquely Chinese use of colour throughout the venue.

The thirty-five Mongolian tent rooms were created out of nine hundred metre-long canvases, each hand-painted with biblical stories. Each tent is unique, and can be modified to create an intimate setting for two people or extended to house parties of up to sixty; they can also be removed to accommodate conferences or gatherings of up to a thousand people.

The Lan Club's international theme is represented by four unique 70-metre-long tables, signifying the countries of India, France, Mexico and China. The Chinese section is filled with golden fish, red lanterns and Chinese herbal medicines and teas. Seventy-five paintings, based on Western masterpieces chosen by Starck and painted by Chinese artists, hang from the ceiling over the tables, concealing pipes and perhaps inspiring conversation (*right*).

Overleaf: The club is on a rented site and may one day move to a different location, so the design is entirely dependent upon furnishing and decoration that required minimal structural alteration. The main challenge was to coordinate the furniture-manufacturing operation, as each piece of furniture is unique. The four Stark-designed black Baccarat crystal chandeliers alone took eight craftsmen two months to complete.

ZHONG SONG APARTMENT AND OFFICE (BEIJING)

Artist and designer Zhong Song is fortunate enough to have an office in the Bai Lin temple, a Yuan Dynasty temple built in AD 1347 in central Beijing. The office space is in the former temple's main hall, restored to its original structure after being modernized as a training centre for the Ministry of Culture.

Zhong's own apartment is a straightforward, minimalist affair, which also occupies a central location in Beijing. Although the apartment was originally on a single floor, Zhong was able to achieve his goal of enlarging it and creating a larger apartment with interconnecting spaces through a multifunctional design and an extremely clever layout. As the apartment was on the top floor of the building, he extended upwards into the gable roof to create additional space. The whole design is unified through a simple pairing of black and white elements.

Zhong's office is in the main hall of the Bai Lin temple, which has important historical links to China's longest reigning emperor, Kangxi (1654–1722). Before he moved into the building, Zhong removed all traces of the renovations carried out by the previous occupant, the Ministry of Culture. In order to prevent further damage to the structure, the office is furnished with desks and workstations that place very little strain upon the building.

By adding an additional floor, Zhong ingeniously turned this small apartment into a two-bedroom bachelor retreat. The steel frame of the black wardrobe provides structural support for the upper level. Downstairs is a second reception and study area (*opposite*).

The mezzanine consists of a sleeping area and a built-in desk (*left*).

The north-facing guest room was originally a terrace under the pitched roof, but was turned into a bedroom underneath a skylight, allowing guests to sleep beneath the stars (*below*).

The simple kitchen opens out – via a revolving door – on to the living room beyond (*above*).

A multipurpose sofa is positioned in front of the kitchen and facing the window; its back is an office desk with a cabinet where speakers and a film projector are stored. Behind the sofa, the tall black wooden structures are used as wardrobes and, in the kitchen, as storage cabinets (*right*).

Another view of the living room (*opposite*).

JINR APARTMENT (BEIJING)

The challenge faced here by architect Jiang Tao, designer of Green T. House and Green T. House Living, was to create a spacious feel in a relatively small apartment, while still accommodating sufficient separate areas for all the usual domestic functions: kitchen, bathroom, living room, bedroom, study room and storage room. Jiang focused on unity of design to create the illusion of space. One way this was achieved was through the concentration of all storage elements in one windowless room, so that the rest of the apartment could be relatively free of furniture. While grey is the dominant background colour, it is occasionally offset by black or more striking tones, such as those of the Italian-style mosaics in the bathroom.

In the bathroom, the cement wall is decorated with iridescent mosaics (*bottom left*). The hue of the tile changes when viewed from different angles and adds a vibrant burst of colour to the small room. A stone bathtub in the bathroom (*above right*). A playful lamp shaped like a bird – produced by the lighting company Luceplan – adds a touch of whimsy to the space (*bottom right*). Seasonal fruits are displayed for their decorative forms within the apartment *(opposite)*.

Translucent white fabric curtains can be drawn completely around the bedroom to simplify the space (*below*).

Grey is the dominant colour in the minimal living room. Although JinR had originally envisaged an all-black environment, designer Jiang Tao used grey instead to avoid an atmosphere that would be too austere (*opposite, above and below*).

Overleaf, left: In the dressing room, Jiang placed rice lights on the black ceiling, which look like stars in the night sky, and make the room appear bigger than it is. A tall chest is placed in front of a mirrored wall; circular holes cut into the chest allow for fleeting glimpses of reflections in the mirror behind.

Overleaf, right: In *feng shui* theory, purple is one of the colours associated with the element of fire and is considered to have energizing potential. In the study, purple is used to encourage creativity and is enhanced by the other bold colours found in the curtains.

HONG LUO (RED SNAIL LAKE CLUB) (BEIJING)

The Red Snail Lake Club is part of a residential development in Huai Rou, 50 kilometres north-east of central Beijing, a district famous for its beautiful natural scenery and for the reservoirs that supply drinking water to the capital.

The architect, Ma Yan Song, had originally worked in the Zaha Hadid studio in London and initially found it hard to get commercial work in China. The client for the Red Snail project, however, recognized Ma's sensitivity to the use of water in his work, and commissioned the building in 2006. The resulting design is a masterful combination of liquid and solid elements. The club floats on Hong Luo Lake, and access is gained by crossing a wooden bridge. The building has no conventional walls and no obvious straight lines, but is a composition of streamlined steel ceilings and glass structures, which make up a teahouse, a relaxation area and a small theatre.

The clubhouse is a public space for the residents of the surrounding community. The building is dramatically sited, hovering over the lake and connected to the land by a wooden bridge, which gives the illusion of being submerged in the lake (*right*).

Integration between the interior of the structure and the external recreational activities allows for an exciting blurring of boundaries. This is also the case with the club's swimming pool, which is enclosed within the lake itself (*below*).

Glass and steel walls and ceilings flow continuously through the
building, creating a sense of fluidity in harmony with the natural
movement of the water in the lake. The layout of the building allows
for easy circulation of the club's visitors and consistently beautiful
views of the surrounding environment.

CONVERSION

Demolishing the old and building the new is a common occurrence in contemporary China. New streets appear in Beijing and other large cities every few months, while whole new satellite towns and cities pop up every few years. In this rapidly changing landscape, where newer, taller and bigger buildings have become the norm, it is refreshing and reassuring to come across the successful conversion and restoration of older structures. The buildings depicted in the following pages are examples of the challenges inherent in keeping the original forms and features of existing buildings, while finding sustainable ways of transforming them into something new.

Although many traditional Chinese houses have been preserved in reasonably good condition, their maintenance is expensive, and some are at risk of destruction. The oldest building featured in this section dates from the late Qing Dynasty (17th century), and was originally located in south China. It was bought by musician, restaurateur and gallery owner Huang Liao Yuan and his business partner Zhang Hao Ming, and moved in its entirety to central Beijing, where a glass and steel restaurant and art gallery were built around it. The resulting new structure is a bold combination of the historical and the theatrical.

The Suzhou Creek warehouse renovation is another successful example of a modern conversion. Suzhou Creek – once a major shipping channel in the first half of the 20th century – had become a dumping ground for Shanghai's industrial waste, earning it the nickname 'Smelly River'. In the last decade, abandoned warehouses and factories lining the riverbanks have been reclaimed and transformed into a thriving community of art galleries, artist and architectural studios, and trendy boutiques and nightclubs. This is due in large part to pioneering architect Deng Kun Yen, who opened his firm in a converted granary warehouse along the river in 1998, starting a trend that others have followed. Deng's continuous campaigning for the protection of older buildings along Suzhou Creek has contributed substantially – in partnership with the Suzhou Creek Rehabilitation Project, launched in 1998 – to the designation of the area as a protected heritage district, and the preservation of more than thirty industrial buildings

from the 1920s and 1930s. This trend towards historical preservation has also spread from Shanghai to other cities throughout China.

Even the unlikeliest targets for architectural resuscitation – the seemingly uninspiring office blocks that mushroomed throughout China during the Communist era – have been imaginatively renovated for residential use. The designer Yang Xiao Ping has proven that such conversions can be functional, fun and creative, transforming what once was a very staid white and grey office into a lively, colourful and spacious apartment, which he shares with his partner Hong Huang, one of the most influential entrepreneurs in Chinese print media.

Preceding page: Big Bird, a 2006 installation at Shanghai MoCA by Yan Jai.

Lights in a Suzhou Creek converted warehouse (*opposite, above left*).

A seating nook at the Pier One boutique hotel (*opposite, above right*).

The illuminated marble bar at the Pier One complex (*opposite, below left*).

Doors at Suzhou Creek (*opposite, below right*).

Z58 (SHANGHAI)

Z58, the headquarters of Zhongtai – a company specializing in lighting – was converted from a former watch factory in the historical French Concession area of Shanghai. Designed by Japanese architect Kengo Kuma, this four-storey construction is an oasis of calm amid the frenetic bustle of the city. The existing warehouse structure was covered with a living plant-wall, composed of steel boxes full of greenery, which surrounds the building with a lush barrier against the outside world.

The ground floor has an exhibition space for art and design shows, as well as for cultural events. The first and second floors house offices and a showroom for the company's lighting products. The top floor functions as a guest house for visiting clients, and includes two penthouse suites, a library, a wine cellar, a cigar room and a gym. The entire floor is surrounded by a water moat, which further invests the building with a unique sense of tranquillity.

Preceding page: One of the penthouse apartments at Z58.

The second penthouse has a louvred ceiling, which can be controlled with the press of a button. The glass roof allows sunlight to flood into the room in the daytime and provides a dramatic view of the stars at night (*opposite*).

The bathroom has a light and airy feel owing to the open design with abundant natural light and the combination of smooth wood flooring and glass doors in a cool colour palate. Rough white stones are under-lit by coloured lights, and in the contrasting artificial light they seem to glow as if on fire (*left, below left and right*).

Architect Kengo Kuma kept the original building's concrete frame and extended it with new steel structures, which are complemented by natural elements such as water, timber, plants and light (*opposite, above left*). Stainless-steel planters filled with ivy form a massive garden shell around the building (*opposite, above right*). The natural movements of the living plants are reflected and magnified by the mirrored steel boxes. Kengo has identified this juxtaposition of man-made and organic elements as a key component of his architectural designs (*opposite, below left*). A cascading waterfall – described as 'Shanghai's Niagara Falls' – flows through five thousand glass rods that were arranged by hand, adding an aural component to the soothing environment (*opposite, below right*).

The bar at Z58 (*above*).

The lobby welcomes visitors into a bright open space where nature has been incorporated into the architectural framework. Kengo describes the building as the 'most living work' that he has ever done; in order to disconnect Z58 from the busy city of Shanghai, he created an urban escape through the use of living plant and moving water elements (*opposite*).

The natural components within the building are often tempered by obvious artifice, as in the rectangular island floating in the middle of the lobby pond. If guests cross over on to the island they find a bespoke wooden bench waiting in lieu of conventional office furniture (*above*).

Another view of the lobby with its tranquil environment. The atrium looks out on to the garden of the adjoining property, which was once the residence of Sun Yat-Sen and is now a museum open to the public (*opposite*).

Water features prominently throughout the building, as seen in the moat-like infinity pool that surrounds the penthouse apartments on the top floor. In the practice of *feng shui*, water elements are believed to help circulate energy, and in offices and commercial architecture water is directly associated with the flow of money (*below*).

The first and second floors of the building are occupied by
the company's offices. The central staircase leads to the
penthouses.

COMMON COMMUNICATION (SHANGHAI)

Founded and run by Li Xue Song, a pioneer in contemporary Chinese advertising, Common Communication is an international film and television company. Because of the number of people – including auditioning actors – who pass through the company's premises, Li needed a substantial space for the office. He was fortunate enough to find a floor in a former 1950s plastics factory. The renovation, which took about four months, has retained the rough factory look and feel, including the original concrete columns. An old shipping container, brought from the Shanghai harbour, connects the lift to the offices. In contrast to such industrial elements, all the fittings are sleekly modern: the power switches were imported from Germany; the entrance system is computer controlled; and the lighting is connected to a motion sensor, which automatically activates lights where they are needed.

The ground floor is made up of a production area, meeting rooms, make-up area and a small photography studio. Within the production area, separate space has been designated for the Chinese team, the European team and the Japanese team. A first floor, added at the time of the renovation, includes a creative department, an IT centre, a library and the chairman's office.

The open-plan office occupies an 800-square-metre floor of a former factory. The ground-floor space is so large that some employees wear rollerblades to move around the office. The dragon sculptures were props used in a television commercial produced by Common Communication (*left*).

Glass display cases embedded in the floor contain photographs of company events and memorabilia from past projects (*below*).

Overleaf, left: An overview of the office space spread out over the ground and first floors. *Overleaf, right*: Several rough elements of the factory have been retained, such as the original concrete columns. Others have been imaginatively disguised: a collage of glossy magazines conceals the ducting systems.

会议室 CONFERENCE ROOM

A 2.5-metre-tall Ming Dynasty wooden entranceway dominates the lobby of the building and is the demarcation for the beginning of the office space (*opposite*).

Another view of the lobby with its eccentric mixture of old and new architectural elements. The shipping container serves as an entrance passageway to the lobby space, transporting visitors in from the outside (*above*).

HONG HUANG APARTMENT (BEIJING)

North-east Beijing is at the heart of the booming Chinese contemporary art scene; it is also an area where the artists and intellectuals of the new China have begun to make their homes in the East German-designed blocks of the Communist era. Hong Huang, CEO of *Time Out Beijing*, lives in an apartment in one such block constructed in the 1950s. Her partner, Yang Xiao Ping, has redesigned the space. Dark, steep stairs lead up to the apartment, which consists of an open-space office and living area and a glass-walled nursery, behind which is a master bedroom. Because this is a rental apartment and not a permanent arrangement, structural changes were kept to a minimum and the majority of the furniture is portable. One dominant feature is the separation of dining and living areas by four rotating iron screens, each constructed of three canvas panels.

The canvas screens used to divide the main room double as raw canvases, which the couple's artistic friends often paint during dinner parties at the apartment. The canvases can then be removed from the frames and taken home as souvenirs.

Yang built the iron coffee table in the living room, and
commissioned the large sofa and day bed for the apartment.
At the far end of the room is the home office (*above*).

Yang also made the prominently featured iron-tree lamp in
the living room (*opposite*).

Overleaf: Neon signs in the dining room cast a warm glow over
the peeling concrete walls, while a collection of framed
photographs complements the shape of a rusted metal fitting in
the adjoining hallway.

DENG KUN YEN APARTMENT (SHANGHAI)

The Bund is Shanghai's famous waterfront, which runs for about a mile along the western bank of the Huangpu River. Long regarded as a symbol of the city and a main tourist attraction, the area has served as a political and economic centre for hundreds of years. Many consulates and banks had their headquarters in the Bund in the first half of the 20th century, and this legacy remains visible in the fifty-two prominent buildings whose architectural styles – including Gothic, Renaissance, baroque and neoclassical – represent a range of revivalist fashions.

Architect Deng Kun Yen has built his apartment in the heart of this area, at the top of the former Japanese consulate. The building was originally constructed in 1905, and later rebuilt after a fire in 1932. Deng's fourth-floor apartment occupies about 150 square metres within a domed structure, with a substantial roof terrace on the northern façade. The south-facing windows are quite small due to the original lofting of the space, so in order to enjoy the views down the Bund, Deng has installed two skylights in the roof. Otherwise, he has been careful to keep structural intervention to the absolute minimum. To enhance the space, Deng painted the walls and beams with limewash, cleaned the columns and doors, waxed the floor and added steel-wired lights to prevent any damage to the original ceiling.

Deng's study occupies a large room on the second floor, which was originally used as a reception room by the consulate, and is one of the most exquisite rooms in the building (*right*). Deng retained the room's original structure, and played up the very high ceiling by suspending red copper pendants from it to symbolize clouds, above a tall screen representing mountains. When the room is dramatically lit, it seems to be transported back to the building's heyday in the 1930s.

A view of Deng's desk (*opposite*). A detail of the wire and white plaster 'mountain' screen (*left*). A detail of the red copper pendant 'clouds' (*below left*). A detail of one of Deng's many antique collectables (*below right*).

The terrace was an outdoor space when the building was in use by the consulate, but had been converted into three small indoor offices in the interim. Deng had all the partitions removed and rejoined the small rooms to create one continuous space (*above*).

Tatami mats – traditional Japanese flooring made of woven straw – line the terrace floor (*opposite*).

The main apartment is on the building's fourth floor in a domed loft space. The arched roof is supported by six classical columns made of sequoia wood imported from the United States at the time of the original construction.

YOU JING GE (BEIJING)

Huang Liao Yuan is an established music critic and part of a first generation of independent music producers in contemporary China. Together with associate Zhang Hao Ming, he opened an art gallery and restaurant in 2003. One extraordinary feature of the building is the incorporation of a traditional 17th-century wooden house in the total design. The building was originally located at a spot near the border of Anhui and Jiangxi provinces. After purchasing the structure, Huang engaged a company specializing in traditional architecture to take the house apart and move it to Beijing where it was rebuilt. It was then covered with a glass and steel construction to accommodate the gallery and restaurant.

The exterior of the art and restaurant complex, including the restaurant You Jing Ge and the Beijing Art Now Gallery *(right)*.

There have been new extensions to the original space, including a larger dining area on the ground floor and more seating upstairs (*opposite*).

Overleaf, left: The owners' art collections are on display in the building.

Overleaf, right: The house, more than 220 years old, has been preserved in excellent condition. The original carved wooden patterns depict Chinese landscapes and local traditions from the southern Chinese provinces. The house originally belonged to an important provincial official.

MAD (BEIJING)

Architect Ma Yan Song is the founding principal of MAD, a youn architectural design firm based in Beijing. The studio's headqua ters are located in a former printing factory near the second rin road in the northern part of the city. Ma transformed a nondescrip industrial building into an all-white, post-modern minimalist spac where MAD architects can present their ideas to clients. I describing the process of designing the office, Ma has said, didn't design much. We just took out everything that was unnec essary – for instance, the ceilings and the wall partitions. Th original wooden beams were revealed when we took down th hung ceilings. Everything above the white area on the walls ha been covered up and in those upper spaces we simply left th bare brickwork.'

The entrance door to the building is at first quite hard to finc Three glass doors face the visitor, making it impossible to knov which one is the actual door. Upon ringing the bell, however, a electronically controlled glass door slides open, leading to a sma gallery room where Ma's architectural models are on display. T the right of the gallery is an open office space. The other side c the building is a large open space, which the firm uses for partie and events, and occasionally rents out for fashion shoots.

The main office is an all-white open-plan layout. Exposed wooden beams descend from the ceiling (*left*).

The entrance hallway between the office and open workspace (*below*).

Bare brickwork was revealed when the original factory building was transformed into the architectural studio (*opposite*).

A large open space in the studio can be used for a range of activities, from relaxing to meeting with clients.

MULLINJER HOUSE (SHANGHAI)

This garden residence stands within the former French Concession area in the heart of Shanghai. Although the house is located on a quiet street, it is only a two-minute walk from the famous shopping district of Huai-hai Road. The neighbourhood is distinguished by a number of former residences of important historical figures, notably those of Sun Yat-sen (1866–1925), the first president of the Republic of China, and Zhou En-lai (1898–1976), first prime minister of the People's Republic of China.

The three-storey, European-style house was built in 1918, when Shanghai was known as the 'Paris of the East'. It had become somewhat run-down over the years, and the new owners – under the direction of architect and interior designer Kenneth Grant Jenkins – were determined to restore the building to its original state, with the additional comforts of modern-day living. Vintage wooden floors and heavy timber beams were sourced from a second-hand market in Suzhou. Craftsmen were commissioned to make exact copies of the original brass doorknobs and window latches. Additionally, replica tiles were imported from a British company, and hand-painted wallpaper was custom-made by de Gournay, specialists in Chinoiserie-inspired interiors. On the outside of the building, a pebbledash finish was applied to provide extra insulation.

The children's bedrooms are decorated in green and pink colour schemes. The bespoke de Gournay wallpaper is based upon 17th-century Western paintings that depict Chinese landscapes, and portraits of the Mullinjers and their architect have been added to one of the garden scenes (*opposite*).

A pair of teak doors with stained-glass panels was salvaged from an old mansion that was being demolished (*left*).

Stained-glass windows are a dominant feature throughout the house, as seen in the Art Deco bathrooms (*opposite and above*). Tiles were produced by the British company Original Style to complement the Art Deco period details of the original house. The picture is a reproduction of a Tamara de Lempicka painting.

PIER ONE (SHANGHAI)

Opened in 2006, Pier One was one of the first boutique hotels and exclusive hospitality complexes in Shanghai. It was converted from the former Union Brewery, which was designed in the 1930s by noted Art Deco architect Ladislaus Hudec. The complex is part of a major revitalization of the Suzhou Creek area, where numerous run-down factories and warehouses have been given second lives as offices or fashionable nightclubs, and the surrounding parkland has been re-landscaped.

The four-storey building has its own private docks and contains four individual venues: the Mimosa Supperclub restaurant, the Monsoon lounge and bar, the Minx nightclub and the Pier One hotel. In Mimosa, an original brewery vat has been retained and a wine cellar and bar have been built around it. The building's original concrete and brick surfaces remain exposed in places along the walls and the ceiling, while sculptural additions visually enhance and soften the materials. Rainbow-coloured circular lights float above the main dining area. The Monsoon lounge bar is located on the top floor of the building, and has an outdoor patio and a roof terrace with daybeds and a jacuzzi, which has superb views of Suzhou Creek and the surrounding park. The Pier One hotel has twenty-four suites in a variety of styles. The uniquely shaped Emperor and Empress suites feature mirrored walls and colourful mosaics alongside soft white furnishings, while the extravagant concubine-themed suite is entered through a copper-tinted mirrored hallway. Many of the hotel rooms have garden or water views, and six Rotunda rooms are completely in the round.

The Mimosa restaurant is at the heart of the Pier One complex. With its 16-metre-high ceilings, the multi-level restaurant is a striking space, highlighted by designer Molis Mao's take on retro decor. Certain features of the original building have been incorporated into the new space, such as a vat from the old brewery that has been converted into the centrepiece of a bar and wine cellar (*opposite and left*).

The reception area of the Pier One Hotel (*opposite*).

The marble bar at the Monsoon lounge on the top floor of the complex (*right*).

The round mirrored bathroom within the Emperor Suite at the Pier One Hotel (*left*).

A penthouse hotel room in a minimal white and beige decor has views of the nearby Suzhou Creek (*top*) .

The Empress Suite features a round bed in the centre of a round room, all in a white colour scheme (*above*).

MoCA (SHANGHAI)

The Museum of Contemporary Art Shanghai (MoCA) is located in central Shanghai within the People's Park, and is surrounded by other cultural venues including the Shanghai Grand Theatre, the Shanghai Art Museum and the Shanghai Museum. The structure was once the park's greenhouse, and the original glass and concrete pavilion, although abandoned, was largely intact when architect Liu Yu Yang began renovating the building. Through a series of additions and adjustments, he managed to convert the existing space into a welcoming public venue, which opened in 2005.

Liu replaced the main entrance with a series of geometric glass structures, and coated existing exposed concrete in dark Mongolian Black stone. Misaligned stainless-steel window frames were inserted into the building's glass exterior wall to break up the slick façade into an irregular surface, as well as to control the amount of direct sunlight entering the galleries. A new roof terrace on the third floor provides a viewing platform for the surrounding park landscape and the densely populated urban cityscape beyond. By surrounding the terrace in glass walls two metres high, Liu has created a sheltered spot for outdoor events.

Inside the museum, 4,000 square metres of exhibition space are spread out over the ground and first floors. The most striking interior feature is a curved glass and steel ramp that sweeps around the original reinforced concrete columns, connects the two exhibition floors and provides uninterrupted views of large-scale installations at the centre of the gallery space.

The MoCA building with its dramatic irregular façade of glass, steel and stone (*left*). The rooftop terrace allows museum visitors a view of the park, and conversely makes events taking place in the space open to public viewing.

Overleaf, left: Metal labels carved with Chinese characters hang above the lotus pond.

Overleaf, right: An exhibition on display at MoCA.

The entrance to the museum (*opposite*).

Visitors resting at MoCA (*above*).

Your Body, 2005, by Xiang Jing on display at MoCA, with a view of Shanghai in the background through the glass walls (***left***).

A museum visitor on the ramp, which connects the two levels of exhibition space and provides an excellent viewing platform (***below***).

TAO APARTMENT (BEIJING)

In response to the owners' wish for a bright, spacious and essentially homely apartment, designer Zhang Zi Hui turned a four-bedroom space into a one-bedroom home. During the three-month renovation period, the clients insisted that they did not want to observe the progress because they trusted the design team completely and wanted to be surprised by the end result.

A long, rectangular living room was created by demolishing the walls of two adjoining rooms. The bathroom, which had previously been small and dark, was connected to the main living space through the installation of a semi-transparent glass wall. The master bedroom was also connected to the living room by a long hallway, which houses a large wardrobe. Sliding doors at the front of the bedroom can be concealed behind two floor-to-ceiling screens, which have been decorated with paintings by Zhang's father.

A wall, covered in wooden floor planks and embedded with lights, faces the main entrance to the house. It is a modern twist on the traditional use of an entrance wall in Chinese courtyard houses to ward off evil spirits. In this updated version, the wall conceals the open apartment space, and serves as the structural wall for a study room behind it.

A view of the open living room. In the foreground is the glass-panelled wall
of the bathroom (*left*).
The bathroom separates the living room from the dining room and
illuminates both spaces with a hazy glow (*above*).

A long, brightly lit wall welcomes people into the house and serves as the structural wall for the home office. There are two doors in this room that can be closed to transform the space into a guest bedroom, complete with an en suite bathroom (*left*).

A detail of copper decoration on a wall in the living room (*below*).

SUZHOU CREEK (SHANGHAI)

In the 1930s, a large number of warehouses and factories were built along Suzhou Creek, which was an important shipping route from Shanghai's port. Many of these former industrial buildings remain along the river, and are, in many ways, perfect structures for architects' studios. Therefore, in 1997, Deng Kun Yen began to explore them as he looked for a place to set up his own architectural practice. He eventually found an old granary warehouse with a floor space of 2,000 square metres, and some of the original Art Deco features of its 1930s construction still intact. The exterior walls are made of China-blue and red brick, while the interior floors are supported by pine pillars, and made of flooring imported from the United States during the International Concession period. During the past seventy years, the building has been used as a granary, a cement plant, a storage facility and a rental workshop space.

Most of the renovation work consisted of removing the additions to the original warehouse. A compressed-air gun was used to clean the accumulated grime on columns and beams, and the white walls were given a traditional lime-water treatment. The floors were partly removed to open up the interior studio space, while skylights were added and south-facing windows expanded to provide additional light.

The terrace of Deng's architectural studio along Suzhou Creek (*left*). The former 1930s warehouse retained exterior ornamentation that has been incorporated into the renovation. Deng was among the first to realize the potential of the abandoned factories and warehouses in this part of Shanghai, and his successful conversion of the space drew a community of artists and galleries to the area. The rejuvenation of the historically significant neighbourhood and Deng's efforts in the preservation of this building were recognized by an Honourable Mention at the 2004 UNESCO Asia–Pacific Heritage Awards.

The inside of the studio is lined with the original imported timber and pine pillars (*opposite*).

A workspace within the studio (*above*).

The studio space was made brighter by the addition of skylights in the roof to let in more natural light (*above*).

Another view of the bright open studio space. The removal and alteration of floors and staircases allows for easy access between the indoor and outdoor spaces (*opposite*).

MIMA CAFÉ (BEIJING)

This café stands within a renovated courtyard inside the Old Summer Palace. It has the reputation for attracting people from the city's art and design circles to this otherwise remote spot inside the north-west stretch of Beijing's fifth ring road. The architectural highlight of the complex is the separate stainless-steel structure housing the kitchen and the striking restroom. It is built on stilts, and resembles the rural bamboo houses found in the Yunnan and Jiangxi provinces in southern China. Wang Hui, the architect, first tried using mirror glass, but found the slightly distorted reflection in the steel to have a more interesting effect.

At MIMA Café, the stand-alone stainless-steel building in the courtyard houses a kitchen and the bathrooms (*opposite*). The entire building is covered by a transparent rooftop terrace, which doubles as a goldfish pond and has a tendency to attract neighbourhood cats. From within the building, looking up at the pond gives the illusion of being underwater: the glass flooring underfoot compounds this sensation. The whole structure is highly reflective and bears more than a passing resemblance to a sculpture. The café's Chinese name – Zuo You Jian – literally translates as 'room between left and right' and represents the architect's hesitation in making design decisions. The English name MIMA – short for 'Mix Maximum' – also reflects the mixture of architectural styles found in the surrounding imperial garden.

The bar in the entranceway is another mixture: more than five thousand books in different languages have been stacked together to create the counter. Triangular coffee tables with mirrored surfaces reflect lights extending from the exposed beams, creating a warm ambience for the evening events, while sunlight casts evocative shadows during the day as guests look out over the courtyard (*right*).

Crossover

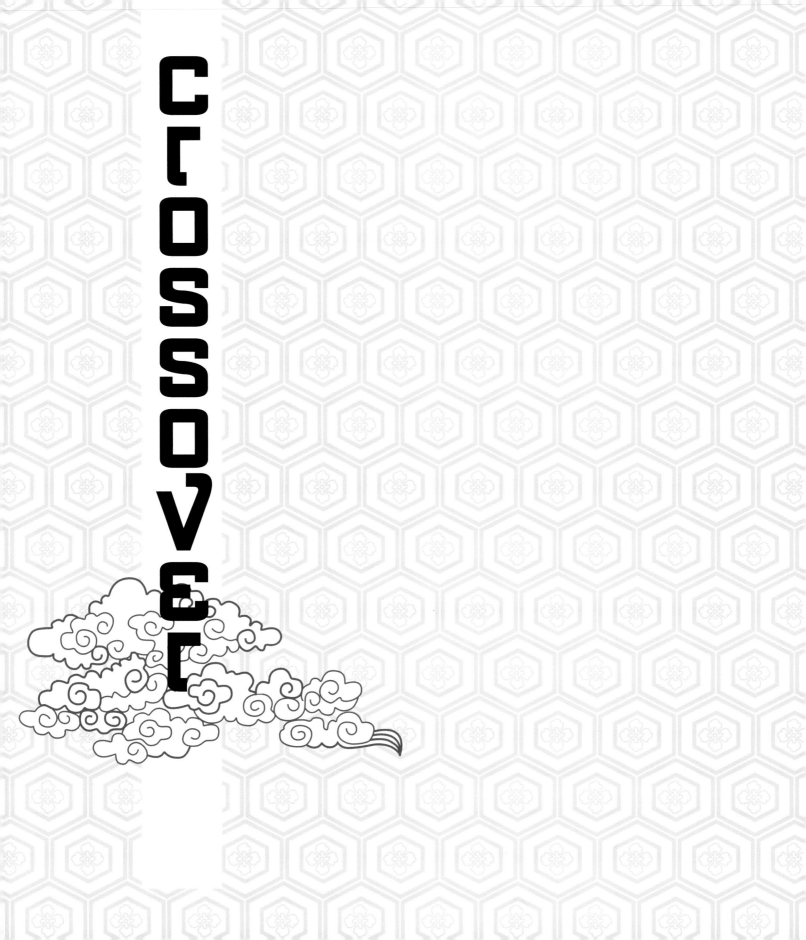

Crossover from one artistic discipline to another has long been a tradition in China. Chinese intellectuals and scholars are often masters of four cultivated arts: *qin*, a stringed musical instrument; *weiqi* (*qi* or *iqo*), a strategic board game; *shu*, calligraphy; and *hua*, painting. The different forms of the arts are seen to constitute a whole and should not be isolated, as collectively they can express an individual's emotions. The arts nourish the mind, and are a path to wisdom, Tao. Seeking harmony between humankind and nature is the essence of Taoism, and embodies the values of ancient Chinese society. *Qin*, an ancient musical instrument, best represents these values, because the sounds it makes balance both loud and soft, fast and slow, high and low, clear and ambiguous, and sad and happy. Chinese music was traditionally used to express a nobleman's state of mind, and promote the importance of harmony. *Weiqi* was historically a game played by scholars and nobles. The simple wooden board, with its black and white game pieces, represents a miniature version of the universe, and symbolizes the ancient Chinese notion of time and space, in the same way that *yin* and *yang* create a unity of opposites. It is believed that playing *weiqi* teaches discipline, concentration and a sense of balance, and reveals the player's character. *Shu* and *hua*, calligraphy and painting, also serve as ways of pursing the divine essence and realizing one's integrity. Chinese characters are among the best examples of multidimensional art forms in the world. More than eight and a half thousand characters exist, as complex combinations of vision, sound and meaning.

Versatility and embracing different disciplines have long been characteristics of Chinese intellectuals, and many contemporary Chinese artists are successful in combining elements of painting, sculpture, performance, design and architecture in their artistic practices. The artist Shao Fan, for instance, has extended his creativity from painting and sculpture to furniture and architectural design, achieving a crossover between the decorative and fine arts. Shao has continued to broaden his artistic explorations to include architecture, and has been commissioned to design a number of buildings for friends. His design for his own home in Beijing illus-

trates the importance he places upon the integration of house and garden, where going from room to room always includes passing through one of his nine gardens.

Ai Wei Wei is another artist who sets no boundaries to his creative territory, working as a sculptor, performance artist, film director and architect. Son of the distinguished exiled poet Ai Qing, he has emerged as one of the most important figures on the international contemporary art scene, and has played a key role in establishing a thriving artistic community in Beijing. For the last few years, Ai has been serving as a design consultant for the Olympic stadium being built in Beijing for the 2008 Summer Games by the Swiss architectural firm Herzon & de Meuron. In summing up the current adventurous mood of the arts in China, Ai has said, 'Design requires strong instincts and a real appreciation of aesthetics, not just in visual terms, but also in terms of right and wrong, necessity or needlessness, and good or evil. The most important questions to ask are who we are, what do we want to do, what do we want to articulate.'

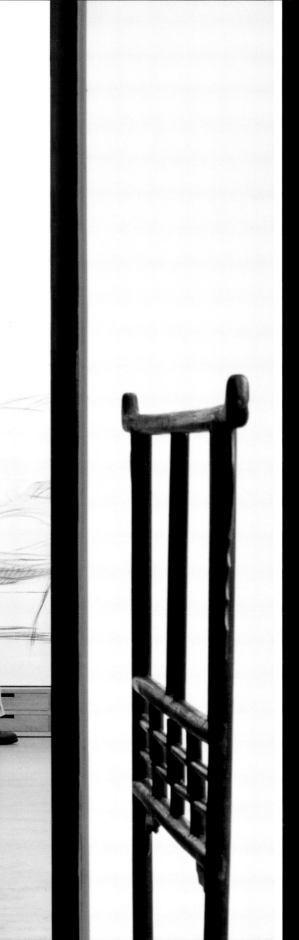

SHAO FAN HOUSE (BEIJING)

Located in east Beijing, this courtyard house was designed by artist Shao Fan in 2004. Shao is a painter, sculptor and designer with a profound interest in Chinese culture, and he drew inspiration from traditional Chinese aesthetics when designing his own home. The building has a minimalist grey exterior, which required two million bricks to construct. The layout of the house does not have a central point; the rooms flow one into the other and there is complete integration of indoors with outdoors. Each room is connected to the next by an outdoor space, varying from untamed jungle-like gardens to paved stone courtyards, and designed with complete disregard for the cold winter temperatures of Beijing. Shao based his fluid indoor–outdoor design upon childhood memories of courtyard houses in the city, and the constant change of surroundings, along with the courtyard view from every room, provides inspiration for his artwork.

Examples of Shao's furniture and sculpture can be found throughout the building, including his various sculptural works based on deconstructions of Ming-style chairs, in which he mixes pieces of antique furniture with modern materials. On display is Shao's most iconic piece: a disassembled wooden antique Chinese chair, reassembled with pieces of transparent plastic.

Shao Fan in his home with pieces from his antique furniture collection visible in the foreground.

One of the nine gardens within Shao's home. The prominence of the gardens in Shao's home is a reflection of traditional Taoist philosophy, which places great emphasis upon a harmonious balance between humanity and nature (*opposite*).

Another garden is paved with simple grey stones covered in moss. The garden designs continue to be a work in progress as Shao allows nature to take over with very little interference on his part (*below*).

The front room of the house – like every room in the building – has a courtyard view. The Ming-style chairs were designed by Shao, and are shown alongside pieces from his collection of Chinese antiques (*opposite*).

This traditional Chinese bed is an important piece in his furniture collection (*below*).

A painting hangs above an armchair converted from an antique chest; both are Shao's creations (*opposite*).

A detail of one of Shao's designs (*top*). The piece is an updated version of traditional Ming chairs, which also number among the collectables within his home (*above*).

The best known of Shao's chair designs is made of a deconstructed piece of furniture, put back together with sheets of clear plastic to form something distinctively new (*above right*). The chair appears to be frozen at the moment of explosion with the wooden elements hovering dramatically in mid-air.

The dining table is constructed of fragments of an antique table held together by plastic components (*opposite*).

The bathroom is another example of a blend of traditional and contemporary elements: wood and concrete have been combined to create a simple unfettered space (*right*).

AI WEI WEI HOUSE (BEIJING)

Artist and self-taught architect Ai Wei Wei designed and built his home and studio on the north-east edge of Beijing in 1999. In the course of a single afternoon, Ai sketched the residence he planned to build. He hired local labourers and began constructing the buildings as a sort of conceptual art project: each day Ai visited the building site and asked five detailed questions about the construction progress. After one hundred days and five hundred questions, the project was complete.

The compound of buildings was designed as a variation on the traditional Chinese courtyard house, and built for a minimal budget with locally sourced materials, which were strictly defined as '130,000 bricks, 180 tons of cement, 7.5 tons of reinforced steel bars, 34 prefabricated planks, 45 cubes of sand, and some wood scraps'. The resulting austere brick buildings are surrounded by high walls. Inside, space is divided by function into an art studio, an office and a large central living area.

Preceding pages: A large garden outside Ai's house is used to display some of his largest artworks.

Simple materials were used throughout the house, which has an open-plan design (*above left*).

A large central space – both living room and dining room – is decorated with furniture designed by the artist alongside traditional pieces (*above left and right, and opposite*).

Large floor-to-ceiling windows dominate the ground floor living space, where the ceilings are constructed of wooden boards that resemble floorboards (*above right*).

Ai wanted the finished house to reveal traces of its construction, and left most of the interior brick walls exposed and unpainted; those that are painted are simply whitewashed to allow more sunlight into the room (*opposite*).

MAO RAN AND WANG JUN HOUSE (BEIJING)

Mao Ran, a businessman working in the interi[or] design industry, decided to play a role in designin[g] his own house when he was visiting his friend, arti[st] Ai Wei Wei, at his self-designed home in north-ea[st] Beijing. When a plot of land near Ai's house becam[e] available in 2005, Mao commissioned the artist [to] design a home on the space. The design proces[s] was very straightforward: Ai simply asked Mao [to] list all of the requirements the building needed [to] fulfil, and within twenty minutes Ai had delivered [a] completed design.

The complex Ai designed meets Mao's desire [to] eliminate his commute and gain control over h[is] working hours by combining office and hom[e] environments. An office for ten people, studios f[or] film editing and dance rehearsal, an exhibition an[d] entertainment space, a conference space and sta[ff] accommodation share the complex with thre[e] family houses, two temporary guest houses and [a] garden for dogs. The buildings are constructed ou[t] of the same grey bricks Ai used on his nearby home[.]

Mao lives contentedly behind the simple brick and cement façades where he has everything he needs for his personal and professional life.

A view of an interior courtyard within the complex.

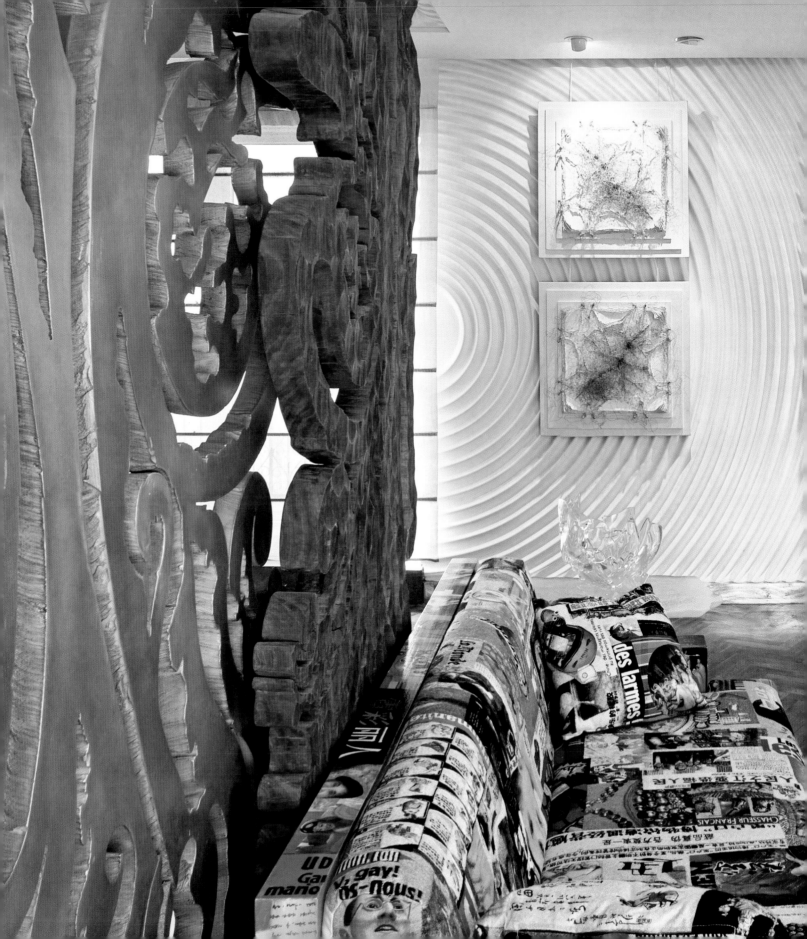

PEARL LAM APARTMENT (SHANGHAI)

Located in the centre of the French Concession area of Shanghai, is Forty-One Hengsham Road, a towering apartment building in a neoclassical style. Pearl Lam's loft apartment occupies the twenty-second floor, with sweeping views of the city below. The entrepreneur and owner of Contrasts art gallery originally came to Shanghai to oversee the construction of the apartment building, which is owned by her mother's real estate development company, and remained living there in order to play a key role in promoting the exchange of arts between China and the West.

Pearl's apartment, with its eclectic mix of contemporary and ancient art and design, embodies this interplay of East and West, and is the result of her own interest in interior design. The apartment is intended for entertaining, and Pearl had all of the interior walls eliminated to create the necessary space. Screens carved with intricate patterns and Chinese antiques, including doors and cabinets, serve to define the smaller spaces of an office and a reception room for the viewing of art. The dining room is dominated by a 40-metre steel table with a thick glass top, designed by Pearl and capable of seating more than sixty guests. The furniture in the apartment includes examples of the Art Deco style specific to Shanghai, as well as contemporary pieces Pearl has commissioned from Chinese and Western artists.

Pearl Lam's apartment is also an exhibition space for both Chinese and Western art. A sofa by Mattia Bonetti is embroidered with images from magazines and pop culture (*left*). A work by Jason Martin is displayed on a heavily textured wall surface (*below*).

The plywood ceiling features cutouts shaped like clouds, and embedded LED lights can be programmed to change the room's colour and mood. The fibreglass and wood chairs resembling spoons were designed by Zhang Qingfang, and the large colourful oil painting is by He Jia (*opposite*). The sofa and chairs in the living room are upholstered in a vibrant animal print fabric. Hanging in front of the window is Sui Jian Guo's *Mao Suit*, which is part of a series of sculptures he began in 1997 (*above*).

The dining room, with its enormous table, is the heart of the apartment and the site of Pearl's frequent dinner parties. The sculpture of a woman's legs, *Eastern Venus*, is by artist Luo Xu.

Mirrors feature frequently in the apartment, where they are used to divide space (*above*). Reflected in the mirror and visible at the far end of the living room, are examples of the carved aluminium screens that Pearl commissioned from artist Danny Lam (*opposite*).

The dramatic red-and-white colour scheme in the kitchen
is used to disguise the room's function (*above*).

A pair of antique doors acts as a dividing wall, creating a
separate space for the apartment's parlour. The chairs are
by Shao Fan (*opposite*).

SUI JIAN GUO HOUSE (BEIJING)

One of China's leading sculptors, Sui Jian Guo, is also the head of the Department of Sculpture at the Central Academy of Fine Arts, Beijing, where he has been instrumental in promoting the appreciation of abstract and conceptual sculpture within China. Sui asked his friend, and fellow artist, Shao Fan, to design a house for him that could serve as home, studio and workshop where he could both produce and live with his artwork.

In Shao's design, all three areas are connected, but each serves a distinct purpose. The workshop has double-height ceilings, while the living area – including bedrooms, a large living room, a kitchen, a laundry room and a utility room – is spread over two floors. The house, like others in the area designed by Shao, uses solar power. The building is surrounded by three gardens, one of which, planted with bamboos and acacias, evokes the paintings of the Song Dynasty (960–1279), and draws attention to the aesthetic decisions essential to Shao's design.

This small back garden has a wooden floor and features a large Taihu rock, which is a common type of ornamental stone used in traditional Chinese gardens (*left*).

Overleaf: Stairs lead from the dining area of the house to the bedrooms. Sui's sculpture *The Discus Thrower* is displayed on the landing.

Multiple versions of Sui's iconic
Mao Suit sculptures (**left**).

A view of the kitchen (**opposite**).

YUE MIN JUN HOUSE (BEIJING)

Yue Min Jun's paintings have set multiple records for the highest prices paid for contemporary Chinese art at auction, but the internationally known artist once lived in the artist village at Beijing's Summer Palace on borrowed money. These days, he is part of a newly prosperous artist community that has sprung up in east Beijing, where he lives in a house designed by his friend, artist and architect Chen Jia Gang.

When Yue commissioned the house from Chen, he stipulated only that the design be modest, simple and functional. Within his home, there are two art studios: a large one for Yue's personal use, and a smaller studio for visiting friends to use. A bright, all-white living room is used for entertaining, and to exhibit Yue's paintings and sculptures. The simple structural design gives primacy to the artwork created on site, and Yue's trademark paintings of smiling, cloned self-portraits are displayed throughout the house.

Yue Min Jun in front of one of his paintings.

Yue's large studio filled with examples of his artwork (*opposite*).

Additional examples of Yue's art can be seen in the bright living room (*below*).

Another view of sculptures and paintings displayed in the studio (*left*).

A balcony on the first floor overlooks the living room. The coffee table was designed by Yue (*below*).

A simple staircase connects the bedrooms to the living room (*opposite*).

WANG JIE HOUSE (BEIJING)

This house was designed by artist Shao Fan, and demonstrates his consistently uncomplicated and economical approach to architecture. Only the most basic materials – grey bricks, cement and wood – have been used throughout the two-storey house. On the ground floor are two reception rooms, a study room, a kitchen and dining room, and two guest bedrooms. The first floor has three bedrooms and an indoor terrace. The design highlight of the interior is the large upstairs bathroom that can be used for bathing and sunbathing. A circular skylight is placed directly above a circular bathtub, allowing sunlight to flood into the white room.

Gardens are an essential part of the design, and surround the building to the west, east and south. The main entrance is on the north and leads directly into a reception room, which contains an indoor fishpond decorated with water lilies in the summer. This blurring of the boundaries between indoor and outdoor space is a hallmark of Shao's architectural practice.

Preceding pages: This 1,600-square-metre weekend home is a typical example of Shao Fan's understated architectural style.

Shao designed some of the furniture in the house. The dining table was made by fusing two wooden side tables with a stainless steel rectangular table (*below*).

The house also contains Ming-style tables, chairs and black lacquer chests from the Qing Dynasty (1644–1912) (*opposite and below*).

A curved *Tiao'an* in the south-facing living room. This traditional type of narrow side table is normally a rectangular shape, so Shao's design challenges the accepted convention (*opposite and below*).

A flower shelf supporting a stone occupies an alcove (*right*).

An indoor pond in the lobby (*opposite*). Across from the staircase is a washbasin made from an old stone sink discovered in an antique market (*right*).

Overleaf, left: The main reception room has a view of the west garden. Shao designed the three different gardens to have a feeling of continuity, yet each one has distinct features.

Overleaf, right: The circular bathroom on the second floor is designed for both bathing and sunbathing.

In one half of the western garden, Shao planted a Japanese flowering apricot tree. This plant is a symbol of vitality because of its beautiful flowers, which emerge in the depths of winter.

ACKNOWLEDGMENTS

Michael Freeman: A special thanks to all the homeowners who kindly allowed me access to their houses and apartments. Some prefer to remain anonymous for reasons of privacy; the others are mentioned in the text accompanying the images. Pearl Lam, who agreed to let me photograph her Shanghai apartment, was a further source of inspiration and help throughout the project. Li Qian did exceptional work in arranging and in a number of cases accompanying me on shoots. Vivi Ying Ho, the Shanghai editor of *Space* magazine, introduced me to a number of new properties. Qin Wen, also in Shanghai, gave invaluable help in shooting Deng Kun Yen's studio, home and conversions. The architects and designers whose ideas and work appear in this book of course made all of this possible. Finally, a particular thanks to Ambassador Guillermo Velez and Martha Uribe de Velez in Beijing for being such hospitable and tolerant hosts on my several visits there.

Xiao Dan Wang: I would especially like to thank my parents Liu Lei and Wang Shi Min for their loving support and my husband Marco Borla for his continuous encouragement and inspiration. Many friends have kindly helped me in sourcing the designs, especially Yin Zhi Xian, editor-in-chief of *Trends Home* magazine, who opened the doors for me to many top Chinese designers. I would also like to thank the following people for their assistance in creating this book: Song Xie Wei, Zhou Yue, Jason Reddy, Wang Cong Yu, Zhang Li Dan, Guan Rui, Zhang Bao Wei, Zhang Zi Hui, Li Qian, Wang Rui Bin, Sahra Malik, Carter Malik, Annette Borla, Zhao Zhuo Lin, Yang Ling, He Zhong Lin, Fan Di An, Li Ying, Qian Zhu, Dang Dan, Dong Jing, Kenneth Grant Jenkins, Karen Wells, Chen Tong, Wang Shu, Sue Shi, Li Hao Yu, Ling Li, Pearl Lam, Wu Peng, Xiao Yong, Zheng Lei, Zhong Song, Yang Xiao Ping, An Lan, Ye Ying, Lu Li Jia, Danio Beltrame, Zhang JinR, Kim Todd, I-Shin Chow, Li Jun, Lu Zhen Zhou, Xu Guang Yu, Lisa Zhang, Jiang Qiong Er, Wei Bing, Song Guo Liang, Yang Yang, Rui Hua Yuan and Sabrina Q.

Xiao Dan Wang can be contacted at xiaodan.wang@yahoo.co.uk.

Baolunge, a Ming Dynasty temple in the Huizhou district, was restored in the 1990s by the American collector Robert Ellsworth (*opposite*).

Pages 262–63: The Pudong skyline at night, across the Huangpu River from Shanghai, dominated by the Oriental Pearl Tower.

DIRECTORY

Hot Loft Restaurant (Beijing)
Lin Tian Mu (designer)
tlintianmu@hotmail.com
Mob: +86 139 0116 0990

Green T. House (Beijing)
Green T. House Living (Beijing)
JinR (owner)
Kim Todd (PR manager)
www.green-t-house.com
info@green-t-house.com
kim@green-t-house.com

Green T. House
6 Gong Ti Xi Lu, Chaoyang,
Beijing, 100027, China
Tel: +86 10 6552 8310

Green T. House Living
318 Cuige Zhuang Xiang Hege
Zhuang Cun,Chaoyang,
Beijing,100015, China
Tel: +86 10 6434 2519

Jiang Tao (designer)
adplan2006@163.com
Tel: +86 10 8046 2638
Mob: +86 135 0118 0369

Deng Kun Yen Studio and Garden (Shanghai)
Deng Kun Yen (architect)
dayang1305@sina.com
2218 Yang Shu Pu Road,
Shanghai, 200090, China
Mob: +86 138 0185 1118

Suzhou Museum (Suzhou)
I. M. Pei (architect)
George H. Miller (principal contact)
www.pcf-p.com
Pei Cobb Freed & Partners Architects LLP
88 Pine Street,
New York, NY 10005, USA
Tel: +1 212 751 3122/4040
Fax: +1 212 872 5443/4041

Pudong Villas (Shanghai)
Rocco Yim (architect)
www.roccodesign.com.hk
RY@roccodesign.com.hk
38/F AIA Tower, 183 Electric Road,
North Point, Hong Kong
Tel: +852 2528 0128
Fax: +852 2529 2135

Fumin Road Apartment (Shanghai)
A 'Lane' House (Shanghai)
I-Shin Chow (architect)
sciSKEW Collaborative
www.sciskew.com
185 Wulumuqi Road, 3F,
Shanghai, 200031, China
Tel: +86 21 6431 9253
Fax: +86 21 6431 6223
Mob: +86 137 6107 3074

US offices at:
601 West 113th Street, Suite 1J
New York, NY 10025, USA
Tel: +1 917 478 0197

People Restaurant – Space 6 (Shanghai)
Sakae Miura (architect)
Germaine Zhou (PR manager)
germaine_zhou@126.com
150 Yueyang Road,
Shanghai, 200031, China
Tel: +86 21 6466 0505

Zhong Ya Ling Apartment (Shanghai)
Zhong Ya Ling (owner)
www.yaling-designs.com
info@yaling-designs.com

A White Apartment (Beijing)
Zhang Zi Hui and Chen Yi Lang (architects)
zfpstudio@yahoo.com.cn
Tel: +86 10 6474 6861
Mob: +86 130 0117 2749

Trends Publishing House (Beijing)
Liang Jian Guo (architect)
Trends Media Group
25/F Trends Tower, 9 Guanghua Road,
Chaoyang, Beijing, China
Tel: +86 10 6587 2515
Fax: +86 10 6587 2500
Mob: +86 135 2192 9998

Huan Bi Tang Gallery (Beijing)
Zhong Song (architect)
hi_zs@163.com
4th Palace, Bai Lin Temple,
Xi Lou Hu Tong, Yong He Gong Road,
Dong Cheng, Beijing, 100007, China
Mob: +86 138 0111 2131

Lan Club (Beijing)
Danny Wang (owner)
http://lanbeijing.com
wangxiaofei@qiaojiangnan.cn
Mob: +86 138 0119 6277

Zhong Song Apartment and Office (Beijing)
Zhong Song (architect)
hi_zs@163.com
4th Palace, Bai Lin Temple,
Xi Lou Hu Tong, Yong He Gong Road,
Dong Cheng, Beijing, 100007, China
Mob: +86 138 0111 2131

JinR Apartment (Beijing)
JinR (owner)
No. 6 Gong Ti Xi Lu, Chaoyang,
Beijing, 100027, China
Tel: +86 10 6552 8310

Jiang Tao (designer)
adplan2006@163.com
Tel: +86 10 8046 2638
Mob: +86 135 0118 0369

Hong Luo (Red Snail Lake Club) (Beijing)
Ma Yan Song (architect)
www.i-mad.com

office@i-mad.com
mad-office@163.com
3rd floor, West Tower, 7 Banqiao Nanxiang,
Beixinqiao, Beijing, 100007, China
Tel: +86 10 6402 6632 / 6403 1080
Fax: +86 10 6402 3940
Mob: +86 139 1189 6627

Z58 (Shanghai)
Chaton Wang (PR manager)
http://www.z58.org
chatonwang@e-zhongtai.com
Tel: +86 21 5258 2763
Fax: +86 21 5258 5758
Mob: +86 135 0172 9213

Common Communication (Shanghai)
Li Xue Song (founder)
http://commonchina.com
info@commonchina.com
3rd Floor, 500 South Rui Jin Rd,
Shanghai, 200032, China
Tel: +86 21 6417 6086
Fax: +86 21 6417 6085

Hong Huang Apartment (Beijing)
Yang Xiao Ping (designer and owner)
Mob: +86 138 0123 3692

You Jing Ge (Beijing)
Huang Liao Yuan (owner)
Huangly0808@vip.sina.com
Mob: +86 139 0106 4663

MAD Office (Beijing)
Ma Yan Song (architect)
www.i-mad.com
office@i-mad.com
mad-office@163.com
3rd floor, West Tower, 7 Banqiao Nanxiang,
Beixinqiao, Beijing, 100007, China
Tel: +86 10 6402 6632 / 6403 1080
Fax: +86 10 6402 3940
Mob: +86 139 1189 6627

The Mullinjers' House (Shanghai)
Sue Shi (owner)
ipp_service@yahoo.com.cn
Tel: +86 138 1680 7101
Kenneth Grant Jenkins (designer and architect)
http://www.jkarq.com
kenneth@jkarq.com
JKarQ Architectural Design Firm
5th Floor, Hong Jing Business Center,
1001 Hong Jing Road,
Chang Ning, Shanghai, 201103, China
Tel: +86 21 6269 0787
Fax: +86 21 6269 0797
Mob: +86 139 0166 1216

Pier One (Shanghai)
Miao Miao (owner)
miaomiao163_163@163.com
Tel: +86 21 5155 8377 / 5155 8388
Fax: +86 21 5155 8398
Mob: +86 138 1787 1708 (Michelle)

MoCA (Shanghai)
Liu Yu Yang (architect)
www.alya.cn
office@alya.cn
Atelier Liu Yu Yang Architects
284 Anfu Road, 3/F,
Shanghai, China
Tel: +86 21 5404 1288
Tel: +85 29 353 2040
Fax: +86 21 5404 2282

Suzhou Creek (Shanghai)
Deng Kun Yen (architect)
dayang1305@sina.com
2218, Yang Shu Pu Road,
Shanghai, 200090, China
Mob: +86 138 0185 1118

MIMA Café (Beijing)
Wang Hui (architect)
Limited_design@yahoo.com.cn
Mob: +86 139 0121 6699

Shao Fan House (Beijing)
Shao Fan (artist and designer)
shaofanchina@yahoo.com.cn
Mob: +86 137 0106 1767

Ai Wei Wei Apartment (Beijing)
Ai Wei Wei (artist and designer)
aixx@sohu.com
Mob: +86 138 0123 7901

Mao Ran and Wang Jun House (Beijing)
Mao Ran (owner)
jingez7406@163.com
Mob: +86 139 1085 0007

Pearl Lam Apartment (Shanghai)
Pearl Lam (owner and art dealer)
www.contrastsgallery.com
Contrasts Gallery
181 Middle Jiangxi Road, G/F,
Shanghai, 200002, China
Tel: +86 21 6323 1989
Fax: +86 21 6323 1988

Contrasts Gallery (second location)
133 Middle Sichuan Road, 5/F,
Shanghai, 200002, China
Tel: +86 21 6321 9606
Fax: +86 21 6321 9605

Sui Jian Guo House (Beijing)
Sui Jian Guo (owner and artist)
suistudio@yahoo.com.cn
Mob: +86 138 0115 4058

Yue Min Jun House (Beijing)
Yue Min Jun (owner and artist)
www.yueminjun.com
yueminjun@hotmail.com
Yue Min Jun Studio
168, Xiao Bao Cun,
Songzhuang Township,
Tongzhou, Beijing, 101100, China
Tel: +86 10 6959 4957
Fax: +86 10 6959 5049